PRAC

Progr

EXAMPLES

Vijay M. Vaghela

Published by Vijay M. Vaghela

ISBN13 - 9789352880003

FOREWORD

The essential design, purposes and objectives of writing and preparing this content matter are to facilitate and assist in classroom teaching. Thus there is not much theory included in this teaching manual, but rather more importance is given to listing examples to be solved along with solutions/ programs for the same. At some places the solutions are not given and it is for the student to find the answers. In most places examples are given with solutions. Thus this manual attempts to focus on the classroom teaching/ learning sequence in a step by step manner, with examples solving, which is a an absolute must for teaching/ learning this subject.

The teacher is required to pose these problem examples in class and initiate students to solve the same and the program answers should not be provided to the student in the beginning itself.

Please note that similarly, if a student intends to use this for reference, the effectiveness of this work will NOT be significant at all, if the student does NOT make attempts to solve and write the programs for the example questions on HIS/ HER OWN. Later he/ she can refer to the answers/ programs provided and check for the correctness or any possible mistakes he/ she might have made. Note that before writing the actual program, the student needs to think and analyze how the problem can be solved. It is possible that the same problem can be solved by using different logic in different ways. Thus the algorithm needs to be figured out initially. Making a flow chart after this would definitely help to understand, confirm and verify the logic that is used to solve the problem/s. Rest, meaning writing of the program is easy and simple...one just need to follow the syntax and the rules of the C programming language!

My regards and best wishes remain with the users of this content, which I hope is useful and beneficial to teachers as well as students who wish to teach/ learn/ understand the basics of C programming in an as simple manner as possible. To students, I can very well assure (through my experience with my students!) that if you sincerely follow what is given in the above paragraph you will not have any difficulty in scoring at least 60% marks in this subject!

Vijay M. Vaghela

Avaliable online at:

www.amazon.com
www.amazon.in
www.flipkart.com
www.pothi.com

ACKNOWLEDGEMENTS

I have been blessed to have worked in the technical education arena at St. Xavier's Technical Institute, Mahim, Mumbai 400016, India for a period of almost 40 years. The institute conducts All India Council for Technical Education (AICTE) approved Diploma Programme in Electronics and Telecommunication Engineering which is recognized by the Maharashtra State Board of Technical Education (MSBTE).

I started teaching various subjects (theory as well as laboratory practices) at the age of 20, having a designation of Assistant Lecturer and through added qualifications, various technical training programmes, and the number of years of experience, presently retired from the same Polytechnic as a Selection Grade Lecturer.

During my entire work experience in the institute, I have had the opportunity to conduct classes and laboratory experiences for various different courses offered in the six semesters of the Diploma Programme, including C Programming. I have also developed laboratory manuals for most of the courses of the Diploma Programme. I express my sincere thanks to Fr. Francis de Melo S.J., Director of Xavier Institute of Engineering and St. Xavier's Technical Institute and Dr. Shivaji Ghungrad, Principal of St. Xavier's Technical Institute for having encouraged me in all my endeavors.

It is of utmost importance here to express my sincere thanks to Mr. Allwyn D'Costa, ex-staff member of St. Xavier's Technical Institute. Mr. Allwyn D'Costa is an expert in digital electronics, computer hardware and networking, programming, numerous application software packages, and he has helped and guided me in the learning of this subject. At the final publishing stage of this book, he has also suggested a few changes and some editing of syntax errors, for which I am grateful.

Your review, feedback, comments, reactions and suggestions are always welcome, which you can send to me personally at:
vagvij@gmail.com.

Vijay M. Vaghela

Practical C Programming Examples

CONTENTS / INDEX

Practical C Programming Examples

DEFINING VARIABES

Defining variables compulsory to be done at the beginning of the program in C.

The basic structure of a C program :

```
#include <stdio.h>
main( )
{
    1. declaring variables
    2. accepting data
    3. processing data
    4. printing results.
}
```

Types of variables are int, float, char

int can be short, signed, unsigned, long (short int is same as int)

float can be float, long float, also known as double

char can be char or string

Variable naming convention can be anything but,
preferably start with alphabet
give meaningful names
if possible put or use underscore (if variable name is long, example basic_sal)

variable declaration

```
        int x ;
        int x, y,z ;
        int a = 0, b = 2, c = 10 ;
int a = b = c = 0 ;    (this is NOT Allowed) (because b and c are not
known i.e. whether they are integers or what…)
```

        instead use
        int a , b, c ;
        a = b = c = 0;

    unsigned int a, b ;
    long int i , j ;
differences between
normal (signed) int, unsigned int, long int and unsigned long int.

normal (signed) int (2 bytes   -32768 to 32767)

unsigned int (2 bytes   0 to 65535)

long int (4 bytes   -2147483648 to 2147483647)

unsigned long int(4 bytes but unsigned will work upto 2 x
2147483647)

float sal, gross ;
float (4 bytes but storage in exponent form from 10^{-38} to 10^{+38} with
7 digit precision. Out of 32 bits 6 may be used for the exponent part
of the number. Since storage is in exponent form larger values can be
manipulated along with decimal places also as compared to unsigned
long int)

long float a, b ;   or   double a, b ;
(8 bytes in exponent form from 10^{-306} to 10^{306} with   15 digit
precision)

NOTE : IN FLOAT TYPE VARIABLES THERE IS NO
UNSIGNED FLOAT

char x; (used for one character and will occupy one byte)

char name [20];   (will occupy 20 bytes AND store a string of 19
characters terminated by '\0' to check for the end of string while
playing around with strings. For example if the name Vijay is stored
in a string variable for which 20 bytes have been reserved, the first 5

2

bytes will hold Vijay, the sixth byte will be automatically be filled with '\0' to represent or indicate the end of the string. The remain bytes in the memory may contain anything which does not matter.)

To accept DATA in these variables proper format specifiers have to be used.

FOR ACCEPTING THE DATA USE :
scanf ("format specifier", &variable) ;

FORMAT SPECIFIERS
format specifiers :

%d	int
%u	unsigned int
%l	long used with %d and %u and %f
	example use %ld and %lu
%c	char
%s	string (of characters)
%f	float
%lf	long float or double

EXAMPLES OF DECLARED VARIABLES :

int age ;
long int basic_sal ;
unsigned int x ;
unsigned long int y ;
float a, b ;
double c, d ;
char sex ;
char name [20] ;

TO ACCEPT THE ABOVE DECLARED VARIABLES USING scanf ( ):

scanf ("%d", &age) ;
scanf ("%ld , &basic_sal) ;
scanf ("%u %lu", &x , &y) ;
scanf ("%f %f " , &a , &b) ;
scanf ("%lf %lf ", &c , &d) ;
scanf ("%c %s " , &sex , name) ;

Note :   1)   ONLY for STRING variable do NOT use ampersand (&).
2)   MESSAGES NOT ALLOWED WITH scanf ( )
3)   DO NOT MAKE MISTAKES WHILE WRITING FORMAT SPECIFIER.
4) KNOW THE WAY OF WRITING THE FORMAT SPECIFIER, THAT IS :   if you have used blank space between format specifiers use blank space (space bar) when entering the two values of data for the two variables. If you have used a comma between the format specifiers, you will have to use comma when entering the data.

PRINTING OR DISPLAYING THE OUTPUT:

printf ("What is your name….?") ;
printf ("\n What is your age…?") ;

                    \n is for new line
                    \t if for tab character

printf ("\n Name \t Age \t Sex \t Qual \t Salary") ;
This will give you on a new line with tabs between the above as below

Name   Age   Sex   Qual   Salary

If you don't want to use \t in the above printf( ) statement, then use printf ("\n Name   Age   Sex   Qual   Salary");

This will produce a similar heading with the specified number of spaces in the printf ( ) statement.

printf ("\n Your age is %d", age) ;
printf ("\n Age = %d Sex = %c", age, sex) ;
printf ("\n %d %d %f %f %s" , age , x , a, b, name);

Note that ampersand (&) is NOT used along with printf( ) statement. Format specifiers are USED in case you are not printing just a plain message.

OPERATORS IN C

Arithmetic operators:

+   -   *   /   %

$x = y + z$ is allowed
$y + z = x$ is not allowed because y, z and x can be
of any type and more particularly this is not allowed because y + z is
not an entity as a single variable.

$x = y + z$ in this the $=$ is an arithmetic
assignment operator
$a = a + b$ can be written as $a += b$

similarly a $* =$ b means $a = a * b$

You can use   +=   - =   * =   / =   % =

Increment operator and decrement operators :

$x = x + 1$ $x = x - 1$
This is same as writing :
x + +   x - -

These are POST increment and POST decrement operators.

+ + x   - - x
These are PRE increment and PRE decrement operators.

EXAMPLE :
If x = 5
a = x + +   will give value of a and x as a = 5 and x = 6
This means do the operation first and then increment
a = + + x   will give value of a and x as a = 6 and x = 6
This means increment first and then do the operation.
    The same is true for - -

a = x - -   will give value of a and x as a = 5 and x = 4
This means do the operation first and then decrement
a = - - x   will give value of a and x as a = 4 and x = 4

RELATIONAL OPERATORS :

<   >   < =   > =   = =   ! =

Relational operators when used in conditions return TRUE or FALSE.

VERY IMPORTANT :
          =   is for assignment
          = =   is for checking for equality

UNARY OPERATORS:
act on one variable (example to change the sign)
          -   x = - a

LOGICAL OPERATORS:
&&   AND
| | OR

Example checking for a condition if

          a < b && c > d
          a = = 5 || a = = 10

CASTING   is for temporarily change the data-type of
                    variable in an expression.
example   (int) 6.5
                    y = (int) x * c;

Take for example a declaration in a C program as :

int a = 8, b = 6 ;
float c ;

After this c = a / b will not work because both a and b are integer type variables.

Therefor use, if required,

c = (float) a / b;   so that temporarily a is made into a float type variable, which will produce the output for 8.0 / 6

This is known as CASTING.......

EXPRESSIONS :

int / int   will give you int
8 / 6   will give you 1

int / float   will give you float
8 / 6.0   will give you 1.33

char c = 'A'   int i = 3
then   c + i will give you 'D'

ASCII value of 'A' is 65
ASCII value of 'a' is 97
                    the difference is 32

Example :

char C = 'A';
printf ("%c" , C + 3) ;   will give you 'D'

printf ("%d" , C + 3) ;   will give you 68

Conditions as below can be used :

if ('A' < 'B')

or
char x = 'c', y = 'A';
if (x < y)

or
char x = 'A';
printf ("%c" , x + 32) ;

the output will be a (alphapet a in lower case)

PRECEDENCE AND ASSOCIATIVITY OF OPERATORS:

Operator Precedence, Associativity and Groups

SR. NO.	OPERATOR CATEGORY	OPERATORS	ASSOCIATIVITY
1	Unary operators	- ++ - - sizeof(type)	R to L
2	Arithmetic – multiply, divide and remainder	* / %	L to R
3	Arithmetic add and subtract	+ -	L to R
4	Relational operators	< <= > >=	L to R
5	Equality operators	== !=	L to R
6	Logical AND	&&	L to R
7	Logical OR	||	L to R
8	Conditional operators	?: += -= *= /= %=	R to L

Example:
a, b, and c are integers then evaluate :
c += (a > 0 && a <= 10) ? ++a : a / b ;

Given a, b, c have values 1, 2 and 3 the answer will be 2

Evaluation of the same if a, b and c have values 50, 10 and 20 the answer will be 5

ARITHMETIC EXPRESSIONS FOR SOLVING:

Evaluate the following:
a, b and c are integers having values 8, 3 and –5

1)	a + b + c	6)	a % c
2)	2 * b + 3 * (a – c)	7)	a * b / c
3)	a / b	8)	a * (b / c)
4)	a % b	9)	(a * c) % b
5)	a / c	10)	a * (c % b)

Answers:

1)	6	6)	3	
2)	45	7)	-4	
3)	2	8)	0	(b/c is 0)
4)	2	9)	-1	
5)	-1	10)	-16	

x, y and z are floating point variables having values:
x = 8.8 y = 3.5 z = -5.2

1)	x + y + z	5)	x / (y + z)
2)	2 * y + 3 * (x – z)	6)	(x / y) + z
3)	x / y	7)	2 * x / 3 * y
4)	x % y	8)	2 * x / (3 * y)

Answers:
1)   7.1
2)   49
3)   2.51429
4)   remainder not defined for float
5)   -5.17647
6)   -2.68571
7)   20.53333
8)   1.67619

Suppose c1, c2 and c3 are character-type variables that have been assigned the characters E, 5 and ?, respectively

Determine the numerical value of the following expressions, based upon the ASCII character set.

E	69		A	65
5	53		a	97
?	63			
2	50			
3	51			
#	35			

a) c1
b) c1 - c2 + c3
c) c2 - 2
d) c2 - '2'
e) c3 + '#'

f) c1 % c3
g) '2' + '2'
h) (c1 / c2) * c3
i) 3 * c2
j) '3' * c2

Answers:
a) 69
b) 79
c) 51
d) 3
e) 98

f) 6
g) 100
h) 63
i) 159
j) 2703

CONTROL STRUCTURES

if (condition)

_____

else

_____

if (condition)
{

_____
_____
_____

}
else

{

_____
_____
_____

}

Brace brackets not required if there is a single statement under if and else.......
Semi-colon not used with if and else........

Examples :

if (age < 45)

if (age < 45 && age > 30)

if (sex = = 'M' && age > 60)

```
if (condition )
        printf ( "True statement" );
else
        printf ( "False statement" );
```

```
if ( condition )
        printf ( "True statement");
```

```
if ( condition )
        printf ( "True statement");
        printf ( "Common statement");
                        printf ( "Common statement");
```

The above second and third printf statements do not belong to the if (condition) and preferably write it without indentation so that it becomes clear that it does not belong to the if (condition).

```
if ( condition )
{
        x = 5 ;
        y = 10 ;
        printf ( x + y );
}
```

```
if ( condition )

      _____
else
{
        if ( condition )
        {
                _____
                _____
                _____
        }
        else    _____

}

      _____
{
        if ( age > 60 )
                printf ( "Retired" );
        else
                printf ( "Not Retired" );
}
else
{
        if ( age > 55 )
                printf ( "Retired" );
        else
                printf ( "Not Retired" );
}
```

```
if ( condition 1 )
{
        if ( condition 2 )
        _____
        else

        _____
}
else

_____
```

Although the same job can be done in one more way, the above method is better than the one shown below.

```
if ( sex = = 'M' && age > 60 )
        printf ( "Retired" );
else
        if ( sex = = 'M' && age < 60 )
                printf ( "Not Retired" );

if ( sex = = 'F' && age > 55 )
        printf ( "Retired" );
else
        if ( sex = = 'F' && age < 55 )
                printf ( "Not Retired" );
```

WHILE STATEMENTS/ LOOPS

```
while ( condition )
{
        _____
        _____
        _____
        _____
        _____

        change the condition parameter
}
```

```
do
{
        _____
        _____
        _____
        _____
        _____

} while (condition );
```

What is the difference between   while   AND   do......while above?

FOR STATEMENTS/ LOOPS

```
for ( i = 0 ; i < 10 ; i ++ )
{
        _____
        _____
        _____
        _____
        _____
}
```

```
for ( i = 1 ; i < 100 ; i = i + 2 )
{
        printf ( "%d" , i );
}
```

16

```
for ( i = 0 , j = 0 ;  i < 10 && j < 20 ;  i ++ , j = j + 5 )
{
        _____
        _____
        _____

}
```

for (; ;)   is equivalent to while (1) , that is, infinite loop.

```
for ( i = 0 ; i < 5 ; i ++ )
{
        for ( j = 0 ; j < 10 ; j ++ )
        {
                _____        Nested for loop
                _____
                _____

        }
}
```

```
while ( condition )
{
        _____
        _____

                while ( condition )        Nested while loop
                {
                        _____
                        _____

                }
}
```

SWITCH AND CASE STATEMENTS

```
switch ( choice )
{
        case 'A' :

                _____
                _____
                break
        case 'D' :
                _____
                _____
                break
        case 'E' :
                _____
                _____
                break
        default :
                _____
                _____

}
```

if (choice = = 'A')

    _____

    _____

else

        if (choice = = 'D')

           _____

           _____

        else

                if (choice = = 'E')

                _____

        else

                _____

*** this is equivalent to the switch on the left.

```
while ( 1 )
{
                _____
                _____
                _____
                _____

        printf ( "Continue Y / N" ) ;
        scanf ( "% c" , & ch ) ;
        if ( ch = = 'Y' )
                continue ;
        break ;
        else
                break ;

}
```

if (ch ! = 'Y')
break ;

SIMPLE BASIC PROGRAMS:

Addition of two numbers:

```
# include < stdio.h >                    header function
main ( )
{
        int no1 , no2 , sum ;        use %f for float

        printf ( "\n Enter first number" ) ;
        scanf ( "%d" , &no1 ) ;

        printf ( "\n Enter second number" ) ;
        scanf ( "%d" , &no2 ) ;

        sum = no1 + no2 ;

        printf ( "\n\n Sum of %d and %d = %d", no1, no2, sum ) ;
}
```

Factorial of a number   5!   5 x 4 x 3 x 2 x 1

```
#include < stdio.h >
main ( )
{
        long int fact = 1 ;
        int no , i ;
        printf ( "\n Enter number whose factorial to be found" ) ;
        scanf ( "%d" , &no ) ;

        for ( i = 1 ; i < = no ; i ++ )

                fact = fact * i ;

        printf ( "\n \n Factorial of %d is %d" , no, fact ) ;
}
```

Alternatively proceed as shown below:

```
i = no;
for ( ; no > 0 ; no - - )

        fact = fact * no ;

    printf ( "\n \n Factorial = %d" , fact ) ;
```

NOTE THAT ALL CONDITIONAL STATEMENTS NO SEMI-COLON TO BE USED EXCEPT FOR

```
do
{
        _____
        _____
        _____
        _____

} while (condition );
```

Program to find the sum of the mathematical series below :

$$\frac{1}{2} \ + \ \frac{2}{3} \ + \ \frac{3}{4} \ + \ \frac{4}{5} \ + \ \text{- - - - - - - - -}$$

upto n terms.

```c
# include < stdio.h >
main ( )
{
        float num , den , sum ;
        int no , i ;
        num = 1 ;
        den = 2 ;

        printf ( "\n Enter how many terms" ) ;
        scanf ( "%d" , &no ) ;

        for ( i = 1 ; i < = no ; i ++ )
                {
                sum = sum + num / den ;
                num ++ ;
                den ++ ;
                }

        printf ( "\n\n The sum of the series is %f" , sum ) ;
}
```

TRY TO WRITE THESE PROGRAMS BELOW ON YOUR OWN:

Program to generate the Fibbonaci series upto specified terms
(the series is : 1   1   2   3   5   8   13
21......)

Program to obtain the sum of the following series (sine)

$$\frac{x^1}{1!} - \frac{x^3}{3!} + \frac{x^5}{5!} - \frac{x^7}{7!} + \frac{x^9}{9!} - \frac{x^{11}}{11!} + ...$$

up to "n" terms

Program to find whether the number is prime number or not :

Hints:
PRIME NUMBER IS A NUMBER
WHICH IS DIVISIBLE BY 1 OR BY ITSELF

check for divisibility by all numbers
check for divisibility from 2 to square-root of the number / (no-1)
check for divisibility by 2,3,5,7,9....upto square-root of the number /
(no –1)

With the first option you are wasting a lot of time (if the number entered is large)
if you do the second one you are wasting less time
the third option does the job in minimum time

WRITE A PROGRAM TO FIND ALL PRIME NUMBERS FROM
NUMBER1 TO NUMBER 2

SINGLE DIMENSION ARRAYS:

They can have multiple locations and in these locations you can store variables of int, float or char type. In the memory the array is stored in a contiguous manner.

char fname [20] ;
This is basically an array whose name is fname and it can store 20 characters (19 + 1) of type character (each character takes 1 byte).

0   19

THE ABOVE IS TREATED OR CONSIDERED AS STRING TYPE.....

int a [10] ;
This is an array of integers storing 10 elements which occupy 20 bytes

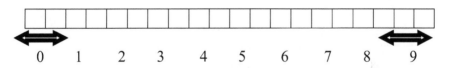

0   1   2   3   4   5   6   7   8   9

int a [5] = { 0, 0, 0, 0, 0 } ;

float b [20] ;   This array will occupy _____ bytes.

The above are examples of one dimension or single dimension arrays.

TWO DIMENSION ARRAYS:

int a [5] [10] ;
You can visualize this two dimension array as below :

0,0	0,1	0,2	0,3						0,9
1,0	1,1	1,2	1,3	1,4					1,9
2,0									2,9
			3,4						
4,0	4,1					4,6			4,9

ACCESSING ARRAYS :

a [5] refers to 6th element
a [3] refers to 4th element
a [0] refers to 1st element

x [1] [5] refers to 2nd row and 6th column element

INPUTTING DATA INTO AN ARRAY :

```
# include  <stdio.h>
main ( )
{
int a [10 ] , i ;
for ( i = 0 ; i < 10 ; i ++ )
        {
        printf ( "\n\n  Enter element number %d" , i +1 );
        scanf ( "%d" , & a[i ]) ;
        }
}
```

This will not change the value of i.....this is to provide a variable message.

PROGRAMS ON ARRAYS:

Program to find the average of 10 numbers entered via the keyboard (store the numbers in an array) and find out how many are above average and how many are below average.

```
# include <stdio.h>
main ( )
{
int  a [10] , i , sum = 0 , lavg = 0 , havg = 0 ;
float avg ;

for ( i = 0 ; i < 10 ; i ++ )
        {
        printf ( "\n Enter element number %d" , i + 1 ) ;
        scanf ( "%d" , & a [ i ] ) ;
        }

for  ( i = 0 ; 1 < 10 ; i ++ )
        {
        sum  = sum + a [ i ] ;
        }

avg = sum / 10.0 ;

for ( i = 0 ; i < 10 ; i ++ )
        {
        if (a [ i ] > avg )
                havg ++ ;
        else
                lavg ++ ;
        }

printf ( "\n Average of inputted numbers is %f" , avg ) ;

printf ( "\n No. above average %d and no. below average %d" , havg ,
lavg ) ;
}
```

> brace brackets need not be used because under this for there is only a single if statement.

Program to print the array elements in reverse order after entering the values in an array.

```
# include < stdio.h >
main ( )
{
int a [ 10 ] , i ;
for ( i = 0 ; i < 10 ; i ++ )
        {
        printf ( "\n Enter element number %d" , i + 1 ) ;
        scanf ( "%d" , & a[ i ] ) ;
        }
printf ( "\n The elements in the reverse order are" ) ;
for ( i = 9 ; i > = 0 ; i - - )
        {
        printf ( "\n %d" , a [ i ] ) ;
        }
}
```

Program to enter 50 numbers in an array, and a number.....and find
the number of times the number is found in the array.

```
# include < stdio.h >
main ( )
{
        int a[50] , no, count = 0 , i ;

        for ( i = 0 ; i < 50 ; i ++ )
        {
                printf ( "\n Enter element number %d" , i + 1 ) ;
                scanf ( "%d" , & a[ i ] ) ;
        }
        printf ( "\n Enter the number to be checked" ) ;
        scanf ( "%d", &no ) ;

        for ( i = 0 ; i < 50 ; i ++ )
        {
                if ( a[ i ] = = no )
                        count ++ ;
        }

        printf ( "\n Number of times the number is found is %d" ,
        count ) ;
}
```

For generalization of the above program :

printf ("\n Enter how many elements maximum 50") ;

You are specifying maximum 50 because you have defined an array of 50 elements by saying .... int a [50] ;

scanf ("%d" , & no_of_ele) ;   You have to declare one
                                               more variable no_of_ele
                                               in the beginning

for (i = 0 ; i < no_of_ele ; i ++)
{
                _____

                _____
}

Program to accept data in two one dimension arrays of same size and store the addition of the corresponding elements of the two arrays into a third array.

```
# include < stdio.h >
main ( )
{
        int a [ 50 ] , b [ 50 ] , c [ 50 ] , i , no ;

        printf ( "\n Enter number of elements maximum 50" ) ;
        scanf ( "%d" , &no ) ;

        for ( i = 0 ; i < no ; i ++ )
        {
                printf ( "\n Enter element number %d" , i + 1 ) ;
                scanf ( "%d" , & a [ i ] ) ;
        }
```

Make one more identical for loop to accept values in the second array where your scanf will scan the values in & b [i]

```
        for ( i = 0 ; i < no ; i ++ )
                c [ i ] = a [ i ] + b [ i ] ;

        for ( i = 0 ; i < no ; i ++ )
        {
                printf ( "\n %d + %d = %d" , a [ i ] , b [ i ] , c [ i ] ) ;
        }
}
```

Program to accept data in two one dimension arrays and print out all the combinations possible from the two arrays. DON'T PRINT THE COMBINATION IF BOTH ARE EQUAL.

1	3
15	40
18	20
20	15
6	45

```
# include < stdio.h >
main ( )
{
        int a [ 50 ] , b [ 50 ] , i , j , no ;

        printf ( "\n Enter number of elements maximum 50" ) ;
        scanf ( "%d" , &no ) ;

        for ( i = 0 ; i < no ; i ++ )
        {
                printf ( "\n Enter element number %d" , i + 1 ) ;
                scanf ( "%d" , & a [ i ] ) ;
        }
```

Make one more identical for loop to accept values in the second array where your scanf will scan the values in & b[i]

```
        for ( i = 0 ; i < no ; i ++ )
        {
                for ( j = 0 ; j < no ; j ++ )
                {
                        if ( a [ i ] ! = b [ j ] )
                                printf ( "\n %d %d" , a [ i ] , b [ j ] ) ;
                }
        }
}
```

MORE BASIC PROGRAMS:

Program to generate the Fibbonaci series upto specified terms
(the series is : 1   1   2   3   5   8   13
                 21......)

```
# include < stdio.h >
void main ( )
{
        int no , f1 = 1 , f2 = 1 , i ;

        printf ( "\n Enter the number of terms" ) ;
        scanf ( "%d" , &no ) ;

        printf ( "\n %5d %5d" , f1 , f2 ) ;

        for ( i = 3 ; i < = no ; i ++ )
        {
                sum = f1 + f2 ;
                printf ( "%5d" , sum ) ;

                f1 = f2 ;
                f2 = sum;
        }

}
```

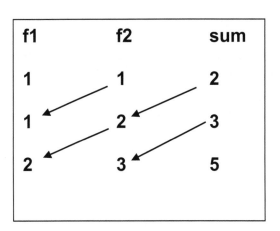

Program to obtain the sum of the following series (sine)

$$\frac{x^1}{1!} - \frac{x^3}{3!} + \frac{x^5}{5!} - \frac{x^7}{7!} + \frac{x^9}{9!} - \frac{x^{11}}{11!} + \ldots\ldots$$

up to "n" terms

```c
# include < stdio.h >
void main( )
{
        int no , i , k = 1 , sign = 1 ;
        float num , den , x , sum = 0 ;

        printf ( "\n Enter the number of terms" ) ;
        scanf ( "%d" , &no ) ;
        printf ( "\n Enter the value of x" ) ;
        scanf ( "%f" , &x ) ;

        num = x ;
        den = 1 ;

        for ( i = 1 ; i < = no ; i ++ )
        {
                sum = sum + (num / den) * sign ;
                num = num * x * x ;
                den = den * ( k + 1 ) * ( k +2 ) ;
                k = k + 2 ;
                sign = sign * - 1 ;
        }

        printf ( "\n The sum of the series is %f" , sum) ;

}
```

SORTING:

		Sequential Sorting	
45	38	25	After this when 25 is checked with 48 and 37 no exchange will take place. After this 25 is left alone, checking starts from 65 which will get exchanged with 45.
65	65	65	
38	45	45	
25	25	38	
48	48	48	
37	37	37	
25	25	25	Because when 38 is checked with 48 nothing will happen but next time when 38 is checked with 37, they will get exchanged. After this 25 and 37 are left alone, checking starts from 65.
45	38	37	
65	65	65	
38	45	45	
48	48	48	
37	37	38	
25	25		65 gets changed with 45 45 with 48 nothing will happen 45 with 38 will get exchanged. After this 25, 37, 38 are left alone....comparison starts with 65.
37	37		
45	38		
65	65		
48	48		
38	45		
25	25		65 and 48 get exchanged, And then 48 and 45 get exchanged. At this point, 25, 37, 38 and 45 are left alone.
37	37		
38	38		
48	45		
65	65		
45	48		
25			When 65 and 48 are compared, they get exchanged.
37			
38			
45			
48			
65			

Program to accept numbers in an array of 50 elements, sort them using sequential sorting method and display the sorted numbers.

```
Define variables
Give suitable messages
Accept the numbers entered by the user into the array
```

```
for ( i = 0 ; i < no - 1 ; i ++ )
{
        for ( j = i + 1 ; j < no ; j ++ )
        {
                if ( a [ i ] > a [ j ] )
                {
                        t = a [ i ] ;
                        a [ i ] = a [ j ] ;
                        a [ j ] = t ;
                }
        }
}
```

```
i is fixed reference
within which
j will vary...........
```

```
After this give suitable messages
and display the sorted elements of the
array.
```

i	j	i	j	i	j
0	1	1	2	2	3
	2		3		4
	3		4		5
	4		5		
	5				

SORTING: Bubble sorting

45	45	45	45	45
65	38	38	38	38
38	65	25	25	25
25	25	65	48	48
48	48	48	65	37
37	37	37	37	65

45	38	38	38
38	45	25	25
25	25	45	45
48	48	48	37
37	37	37	48
65	65	65	65

38	25	25
25	38	38
45	45	37
37	37	45
48	48	48
65	65	65

25	25	25
38	37	37
37	38	38
45	45	45
48	48	48
65	65	65

1
2
3
4
5
6

During the check when it finds that no transaction / exchange has taken place it will come out of the loop. If the numbers are already in an almost sorted manner, it will be able to finish the job of sorting fast and come out of the loop. In sequential sorting, it will go through all the loops regardless of whether the elements are already sorted or in an almost sorted condition. Therefore bubble sorting is much better / faster than sequential sorting particularly while dealing with large number of elements (and especially if they are in an almost sorted condition).

Program to accept numbers in an array of 50 elements, sort them using bubble sorting method and display the sorted numbers.

Define variables
Give suitable messages
Accept the numbers entered by the user into the array

```
flag = 1;

while ( flag )
{
        flag = 0 ;
        for ( i = 0 ; i < no – 1 ; i ++ )
        {
                if ( a [ i ] > a [ i + 1 ] )
                {
                        t = a [ i ] ;
                        a [ i ] = a [ i + 1 ] ;
                        a [ i + 1 ] = t ;
                        flag = 1 ;
                }
        }
}
```

for flag = 1

while flag = 1

flag = 0

for

flag = 1

PROGRAMS ON TWO DIMENSION ARRAYS:

Program to store a multiplication table in a 2 dimension array as shown below (and also display/ print the output):

1	2	3	4	5	6	7	8	9	10
2	4	6	8	10	12	14	16	18	20
3	6	9	12	15	18	21	24	27	30
4	8	12							
5	10	15	20						
6	12	18							
7	14								
8	16								
9									
10	20	30	40						100

```
# include < stdio.h >
main ( )
{
        int a [ 10 ] [ 10 ] , i , j ;

        for ( i = 0 ; i < 10 ; i ++ )
        {
                for ( j = 0 ; j < 10 ; j ++ )
                {
                        a [ i ] [ j ] = ( i + 1 ) * ( j + 1 ) ;
                }
        }
        for ( i = 0 ; i < 10 ; i ++ )
        {
                printf ( "\n" ) ;
                for ( j = 0 ; j < 10 ; j ++ )
                {
                        printf ( "%5d" , a [ i ] [ j ] ) ;
                }
        }
}
```

Program to find row sum and column sum and print in proper formatted way. The user will decide number of rows and columns and also enter the values. The output should be as shown below considering 4 rows and 5 columns:

	0,0	0,1	0,2	0,3	0,4	0,5	
0,0	1	5	1	8	2	17	0,5
1,0	2	6	2	7	1	18	1,5
2,0	3						2,5
3,0	4						3,5
4,0	10						

4,0   4,1   4,2   4,3   4,4

```
#include < stdio.h >
main ( )
{
        int a [ 100 ] [ 100 ] , i , j , rows , cols ;

        printf ( "\n Enter no. of rows and cols....max 99 ) ;
        scanf ( "%d %d" , &rows , &cols ) ;

        for ( i = 0 ; i < rows ; i ++ )
        {
                for ( j = 0 ; j < cols ; j ++ )
                {
                  printf ( "\n Enter value for row %d and col %d" i+1 ,
                  j +1 ) ;
                   scanf ( "%d" , &a [ i ] [ j ] ) ;
                }
        }

        for ( i = 0 ; i < rows ; i ++ )
                a [ i ] [ cols ] = 0 ;
```

0,5 1,5 2,5 3,5
are filled with zero....
cols is fixed

```
        for ( j = 0 ; j < cols ; j ++ )
                a [ rows ] [ j ] = 0 ;
for ( i = 0 ; i < rows ; i ++ )
{
```

4,0 4,1 4,2 4,3 4,4
are filled with zero...
rows is fixed

row fixed , column changes

```
        for ( j = 0 ; j < cols ; j ++ )
        {
                a [ i ] [ cols ] = a [ i ] [ cols ] + a [ i ] [ j ] ;
        }
}

for ( j = 0 ; j < cols ; j ++ )
{
        for ( i = 0 ; i < rows ; i ++ )        column fixed , row changes
        {
                a [rows] [ j ] + = a [ i ] [ j ] ;
        }
}
```

> **Instead of the above two nested for loops, job of getting totals can be done with a single nested for loop :**
>
> ```
> for ( i = 0 ; i < rows ; i ++ )
> {
>         for ( j = 0 ; j < cols ; j ++ )
>         {
>                 a [ i ] [ cols ] + = a [ i ] [ j ] ;
>                 a [ rows ] [ j ] + = a [ i ] [ j ] ;
>         }
> }
> ```

The last job is to display the output as follows :

```
for ( i = 0 ; i < = rows ; i ++ )
{
        printf ( "\n" ) ;
        for ( j = 0 ; j < = cols ; j ++ )
        {
                        printf ( "%d" , a [ i ] [ j ] ) ;
                }
        }
}
```

STRINGS, STRING FUNCTIONS AND RELATED PROGRAMS:

char name [20] ;   name is a variable (string type)
format specifier %s and preferably   use gets instead of scanf
                                use puts instead of printf
char name [10] [20] will store 10 names of 20 characters each
(actually 19)

With strings there are a lot of functions:
Some of the frequently required and used are:

strcmp (s1 , s2)   DO NOT USE   if (s1 = = s2)

strcpy (s1 , s2)   DO NOT USE   s1 = s2 ;

strlen (s)   to find the length of the string

FOR THE ABOVE YOU HAVE TO   #include < string.h >

tolower (c)
toupper (c)
islower (c)
isupper (c)

FOR THESE YOU HAVE TO   #include < ctype.h >

Write a program to accept 10 names and sort them alphabetically and display the sorted list.
Vijay, Vijvag, Albert, Ramesh, Ila, Neeta, Robert.........

```
#include < stdio.h >
#include < string.h >
main ( )
{
        char name [10][20] , temp [20] ;
        int i , j ;

        for ( i = 0 ; i < 10 ; i ++ )
        {
                printf ( "\n Enter name of person number %d" , i + 1 )
                ;
                gets ( name [ i ] ) ;
        }
```

SEQUENTIAL SORTING:

```
        for ( i = 0 ; i < 9 ; i ++ )
        {
                for ( j = i + 1 ; j < 10 ; j ++ )
                {
                        if ( strcmp ( name [ i ] , name [ j ] ) > 0 )
                        {
                                strcpy ( temp , name [ i ] ) ;
                                strcpy ( name [ i ] , name [ j ] ) ;
                                strcpy ( name [ j ] , temp ) ;
                        }
                }
        }

        for ( i = 0 ; i < 10 ; i ++ )
                puts ( name [ i ] ;
}
```

Program to enter a string of maximum 50 characters and enter a single character AND find out how many times the character is found in the string.

```
# include < stdio.h >
main ( )
{
        char string [50] ;
        int i ;
        char x ;
        int ctr = 0 ;

        printf ( "\n Enter the string" ) ;
        scanf ( "%s" , string ) ;
        gets (string) ;
        printf ( "\n Enter the character to be searched for" ) ;
        scanf ( "%c" , &x ) ;

        for ( i = 0 ; string [ i ] ! = '\0' ; i ++ )
        {
              if (string [ i ] = = x )
                    ctr ++ ;
        }

        printf ( "\n The character is found %d" , ctr ) ;
}
```

scanf( ) space is the terminator **BETTER** to use: **gets(string); Use either scanf or gets on the left - NOT BOTH!**

i < 50 may find some nonsense in memory which may correspond to a match and the answer can come wrong.

Brace brackets not necessary because of a single if.

INSTEAD OF SAYING

                           string [i] ! = '\0'

YOU CAN USE

                           string [i]

WHICH MEANS AS LONG AS THE STRING IS THERE GO ON DOING THE JOB INSIDE THE LOOP......

Program to enter a string of maximum 50 characters and enter a single character AND find out how many times the character is found in the string.

```
# include < stdio.h >
main ( )
{
        char string [50] ;
        int i ;
        char x ;
        int ctr = 0 ;

        printf ( "\n Enter the string" )
        scanf ( "%s" , string ) ;
        gets (string) ;
        printf ( "\n Enter the character to be searched for" ) ;
        scanf ( "%c" , &x ) ;

        for ( i = 0 ; string [ i ] ! = '\0' ; i ++ )
        {
                if (string [ i ] = = x )
                        ctr ++ ;
        }

        printf ( "\n The character is found %d" , ctr ) ;
}
```

scanf( ) space is the terminator **BETTER** to use: **gets(string); Use either scanf or gets on the left - NOT BOTH!**

i < 50 may find some nonsense in memory which may correspond to a match and the answer can come wrong.

Brace brackets not necessary because of a single if.

INSTEAD OF SAYING

string [i] ! = '\0'

YOU CAN USE

string [i]

WHICH MEANS AS LONG AS THE STRING IS THERE GO ON DOING THE JOB INSIDE THE LOOP......

Program to accept a string and convert it to lowercase:

```
# include < stdio.h >
main ( )
{
char name [20] ;
int i ;
printf ( "\n Enter your name" ) ;
gets (name);
for ( i = 0 ; name [ i ] ! = '\0' ; i ++ )
{
        if  (name [ i ] > = 'A' && name [ i ] < = 'Z' )
                name [ i ] = name [ i ] + 32 ;
}
printf ( "\n Converted to lower case is %s" , name ) ;
}
```

> i < 20 would have worked because in the end while printing in lower case it would have stopped at \0 . In the next example it will not work....you have to use : name [i] ! = ' \0 '

> Scanf ( ) ....
> ....space is terminator and hence gets ( ) is better.
> ' \0 ' is termination for string.

include < ctype.h >   this header file contains functions for strings.
Then instead of if statement above you can use
        name [i] = tolower (name [i]) ;
This function works on single character and so for loop is required.

Program to reverse a string, the reversed string is put in a new or different string:

```
# include < string.h >
# include < stdio.h >
main ( )
{
        char str1 [100] , str2 [100] ;
        int i , j , l ;

        printf ( "\n Enter a string" ) ;
        gets (str1) ;

        l = strlen (str1) ;

        for ( i = 0 ; i < l ; i ++ )
        {
                str2 [ i ] = str1 [ l - i - 1 ] ;
        }

        str2 [ i ] = ' \ 0 ' ;            or use  str2 [ l ] = ' \0 ' ;

        puts (str2) ;

}
```

```
                         0                    9

                       a b c d e f g h i j '\0'
```

```
for ( i = l - 1 ; i > = 0 ; i - - )
{
        str2 [ l - i - 1 ] = str1 [ i ] ;
}
str2 [ l ] = ' \0 ';
```

10 - 9 - 1	
l - i -1	i
0	9
1	8
2	7
	6

Program to reverse a string and the reversed string is kept in the same string (do not use a separate string to put the reversed string)

```
# include < stdio.h >
# include < string.h >
main ( )
{
        char str1 [100] , temp ;
        int i , j ;
        int len;
        printf ( "\n Enter a string " ) ;
        gets (str1) ;

        len = strlen (str1) ;

        for ( i = 0 ; i < 1 / 2 ; i ++ )
        {
                temp = str1 [ i ] ;
                str1 [ i ] = str1 [ len - i - 1 ] ;
                str1 [ len - i -1 ] = temp ;
        }

        puts (str1) ;

}
```

i	1 - i -1
0	4
1	3
2	2
3................	
a b c d e	
e b c d a	
e d c b a	

Program to join 2 strings and put in a 3rd string

str1	vijay	
str2	vaghela	**str3 = str1 + str2**
str3	vijay vaghela	

```c
# include < stdio.h >
main ( )
{
        char str1[50] , str2[50] , str3[100] ;
        int i , j ;

        printf ("Enter two strings ) ;
        gets (str1) ;
        gets (str2) ;

        for ( i = 0 ; str1[ i ] ; i ++ )
        {
                str3[ i ]  = str1[ i ] ;
        }
        str3[ i ] = " " ;      str3[ i ++ ] = " " ;
        i ++ ;

        for ( j = 0 ; str2 [ j ] ; j ++ , i ++ )
        {
                str3 [ i ] = str2 [ j ] ;
        }

        str3 [ i ] = '\0' ;
        puts (str3) ;
}
```

Program to join 2 strings, the second string should be added to the first string so that the first string will finally have the content of both the strings,

that is   **str1 = str1 + str2**


```c
# include <stdio.h >
main ( )
{
        char str1[100] , str2[50] ;
        int i , j ;

        printf ( "\n Enter first string max 50 characters" ) ;
        gets (str1) ;
        printf ( "\n Enter second string max 50 characters" ) ;
        gets (str2) ;

        for ( i = 0 ; str1[ i ] ; i ++ );

        str1[ i ++ ] = " " ;

        for ( j = 0 ; str2[ j ] ; j ++ , i ++ )
        {
                str1[ i ] = str2[ j ] ;
        }

        str1[ i ] = '\0' ;

        puts (str1) ;
}
```

Vijay M. Vaghela

Program to accept a string and find out if it is a palindrome or not.

```
# include <stdio.h >
main ( )
{
        char str1[100] ;
        int i, flag ;
        int len;

        printf ("\n Enter a string" ) ;
        gets (str1) ;

        len = strlen(str1) ;
        flag = 0 ;

        for ( i = 0 ; i < len / 2 ; i ++ )
        {
                if ( str1[ i ] ! = str1[ len - i - 1 ] )
                        flag = 1 ;
        }

        if ( flag = 1 )
                printf ( "String is NOT a palindrome ) ;
        else
                printf ( "String is a palindrome ) ;
}
```

```
for ( i = 0 ; i < len / 2 ; i ++ )
{
        if ( str1[ i ] ! = str1[ len - i - 1 ] )
                printf ( "Not a palindrome" ) ;
        else
                printf ( "A palindrome" ) ;
}

printf ( " A palindrome" ) ;
```

49

Enter text any amount 1 line / 5 lines / 5 pages. Find the number of characters, words and lines.

```
# include <stdio.h>
main ( )
{
        int ch , c = 0 , w = 0 , l = 0 ;

        while ( (ch = getchar( ) ) ! = EOF )
        {
                c ++ ;
                if ( ch = = ' ' )
                        w ++ ;
                if ( ch = = '\n' )
                {
                        l ++ ;
                        w ++ ;
                }
        }

        printf ("\n Chars = %d , Words = %d , lines = %d" , c , w , l )
        ;
}
```

> **(F6) ^Z terminator**
>
> EOF
>
> **(-1)**

What about multiple '\n' …. in the above program?

```
if ( ch = = '\n' )
{
        l ++ ;
        if ( prevch ! = '\n' )
                w ++ ;
}
```

What about multiple blanks …. in the above program?

```
int prevch = ' x ' ;

        while ( ( ch = getchar( ) ) ! = EOF )
        {
                c ++ ;
                if ( ch = = '\n' )
                {
                        l ++ ;
                        w ++ ;
                }
                if ( prevch ! = ' ' && ch = = ' ' )
                        w ++ ;

                prevch = ch ;
        }
```

FUNCTIONS AND POINTERS WITH SIMPLE EXAMPLE

```
void main ( )
{
        print_header ( ) ;
        accept data ( ) ;              could be for 3 arrays
        calculate ( ) ;
        print_title ( ) ;
print_details ( ) ;
)

void print_header ( )
{
        ═══════════
        ═══════════
}       ═══════════

void accept_data ( )
{
        ═══════════
        ═══════════
        ═══════════
}

void calculate ( )
{
        ═══════════
        ═══════════
}       ═══════════

void print-title ( )
{
        ═══════════
        ═══════════
        ═══════════
}
void print_details ( )
{
```

}

* Functions help to avoid repeating code

* The structure of program becomes modular

* after calculating / processing a function will return value

* if there is no return value you must specify void

* if there is return value, specify the data type returning

* a function will return only one value

EXAMPLE:

```
void main ( )
{
        int a [100] ;

        print_header ( ) ;
        accept_data (a) ;
        sorting (a) ;
        print_title ( ) ;
        print_details (a) ;
}

void print_header ( )
{
        clrscr ( );
        printf ("\n\n Enter the data in the array of 100 elements" ) ;
        printf ("\n\n ) ;
}

void accept-data (a)
{
        int i ;
        for ( i = 0 ; i < 100 ; i ++ )
        {
                scanf ( "%d" , & a[ i ] ) ;
        }
}

void print_title ( )
{
        clrscr ( ) ;
        printf ( "\n\n The array elements in sorted order are" ) ;
        printf ( "\n\n" ) ;
}
```

```
void print_details ( )
{
        int i ;
        for ( i = 0 ; i < 100 ; i ++ )
                printf ( "%d" , a [ i ] ) ;
}

void sorting (a)
{
        int i , j ;

        for ( i = 0 ;  i < 99 ; i ++ )
        {
                for ( j = i + 1 , j < 100 ; j ++ )
                {
                        if ( a [ i ] > a [ j ] )
                        {
                                t = a [ i ] ;
                                a [ i ] = a [ j ] ;
                                a [ j ] = t ;
                        }
                }
        }
}
```

DATA HANDLING IN A FUNCTION

IMPORTANT ......The data in a function is local to that function and gets lost when the function execution is over.

Therefore we have to pass variables by reference (parameter or argument) and not by value if we want to return the data AND THIS IS WHERE POINTERS COME IN.

A pointer is a variable which holds the address of another variable and NOT THE CONTENTS OF VARIABLE.

The pointer type is the same as the variable it is pointing to.

```
int x ;
int *p = &x ;

x = 55 ;
printf ( "%d" , x ) ;    55
printf ( "%d" , *p ) ;   55
printf ( "%d" , &x ) ;   1025
printf ( "%d" , p ) ;    1025
```

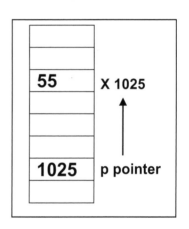

p   is referring to the pointer   1025
*p   is referring to data stored at that pointer location (data or contents at location 1025 which is 55

```
void main ( )
{
        int a, b ;
        printf  ("\n Enter the values for a and b" ) ;
        scanf ( "%d %d" , &a , &b ) ;

        swap ( a, b ) ;

        printf ( "\n %d %d" , a , b ) ;
}

void swap (int a , int b )
{
        int t ;
        t = a ;
        a = b ;
        b = t ;
}
```

```
swap ( &a , &b ) ;
printf ( "\n %d %d , a , b ) ;
}

void swap (int * a , int *b )
{
        int t ;
        t = *a ;
        *a = *b ;
        *b = t ;
}
```

If a = 5 and b = 10

WHEN PRINTING PASSING BY VALUE WILL GIVE a = 5 and b = 10	WHEN PRINTING PASSING BY REFERENCE WILL GIVE a = 10 and b = 5

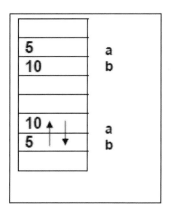 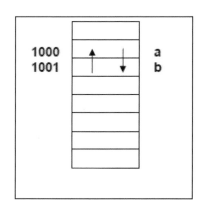

```
int x, y ;
char ch , str[100] ;
float a , b ;

int *x1 , *y1 ;
char *ch1 , *str1 ;
float *a1 , *b1 ;
x1 = &x ;               y1 = &y ;
a1 = &a ;               b1 = &b ;
ch1 = &ch ;             str1 = str ;

scanf ( "%d %d" , &x , &y ) ;
          or you can use
scanf ("%d %d" , x1 , y1 ) ;
```

pointer name refers to address *pointer name refers to the contents of variable pointed to by pointer variable.

POINTER ARITHMETIC AND RELATED PROGRAMS:

INTEGER TYPE   if x1 refers to 1025
x1 + 1 will refer to 1027

FLOAT TYPE   if a1 refers to 1045
a1 + 1 will refer to 1049

CHARACTER TYPE if ch1 refers to 2000
ch1 + 1 will refer to 2001

STRING TYPE   if str1 refers to 3000
str1 + 5 will refer to 3005

Using pointers in just one single program consisting of only main ( ) is meaningless or useless since the job can be done any way. Pointers are useful, essential and will have a meaningful use when incorporated with programs with functions.

The variables defined in a function disappear from memory once the function has been executed and you are out of the function.

The variables defined in main ( ) and in function ( ) are separate and do not have any relationship or are not related or there is no relation between them.

IN GENERAL......
PASSING BY VALUE MAY BE USED only 1 % of the time in programs.
PASSING BY REFERENCE one will come across 99% of the time.

ACCEPTING DATA IN AN ARRAY:

```
void main ( )
{
        int a[100] ;
        accept_data (a) ;
}
void accept_data ( int a[100] )
{
        int i ;
        for ( i = 0 ; i < 100 ; i ++ )
        {
                scanf ( "%d" , &a [ i ] ) ;
        }
}
```

```
void accept_data (a)
int a [ 100 ] ;
{

        _____
        _____
        _____
        _____
        _____

}
```

Accept data in an array. Accept a number. Find out how many times the number is found in the array.

```
void main ( )
{
        int a[10], b, c ;
        accept_data ( a , &b ) ;
        c = find_times(a , b) ;
        printf( "%d" , c ) ;
}
```

int a[10]
Then a represents the base address or starting address of the array which is equivalent to &a[0]

```
void accept_data( int *a1 , int *b1 )
{
        int i ;
        for ( i = 0 ; i < 10 ; i ++ )
                scanf ("%d" , (a1 + i ) ) ;
        scanf ("%d" , b1 ) ;
}
```

by reference

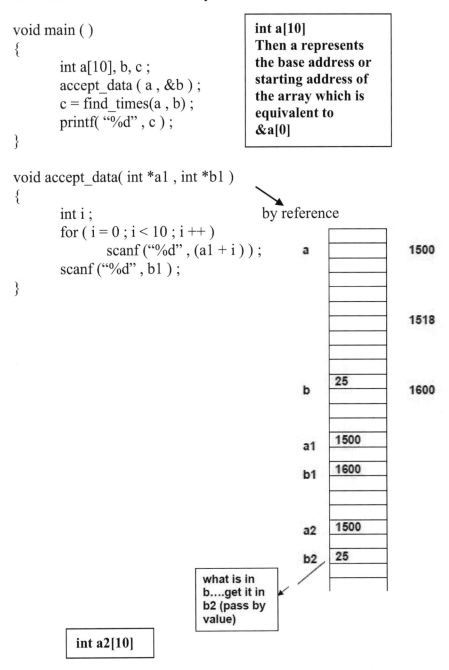

int a2[10]

```
int find_times ( int * a2 , int b2 )

{
        int i , d = 0 ;
        for ( i = 0 ; i < 10 ; i ++ )
        {
                if ( *a2 ++ = = b2 )
                        d ++ ;
        }
        return (d) ;
}
```

if (a [i] = = b2)

or you can use…..
```
                if ( *(a2 + i ) = = b2 )
```

pointer a1 is pointing or referring to the starting address of array a which means a1 contains 1500 and from this point onwards by incrementing the address or pointer we are putting data in the array up to 1518.

pointer b1 contains 1600 which means at location 1600 put 25 since we are passing by reference in the first part when accepting data.

when checking in the second part array contents passed by reference, b2 passed by value…..could have been passed by reference but not required.

Program to accept 10 + 10 numbers in two arrays and get the sum of
the corresponding elements in a third array.

```
void main ( )
{
        int a [10] , b [10] , c [10] ;
        accept_data ( a ) ;
        accept_data ( b) ;
        sum ( a , b , c ) ;
        print ( a , b , c ) ;
}
void accept_data (int *x)
{
        int i ;
        for ( i = 0 ; i < 10 ; i ++ )
                scanf ( "%d" , x ++ ) ;
}
void sum ( int a[10] , int b[10] , int *c )
{
        int i ;
        for ( i =0 ; i < 10 ; i ++ )
                *c++ = a [ i ] + b [ i ] ;
}
```

example:
starting address of a   1000
starting address of b   2000
starting address of c   3000
then
pointer x will have 1000 when starting (and passing) entering data in array a

pointer x will have 2000 when starting (and passing) entering data in array b

pointer c will be pointing to the starting address of c and will start passing the summed values to address 3000 onwards

passed by value, data exists and changes are not going to take place

If you had passed all by reference and used
*c++ = *a++ + *b++ ;
it would take less memory usage but more time for processing because of going around in circles

```
void print ( int *a , int *b , int *c )
{
        int i ;
        for ( i = 0 ; i < 10 ; i ++ )
        {
        printf ( "%d + %d = %d" , *a++ , *b++ , *c++ ) ;
        }
}
```
OR YOU CAN USE *(a + i) , * (b + i) , * (c + i)

STRING PROGRAMS USING POINTERS

A function to copy string 2 to string 1. Since this function strcpy ( ) already exists in C language, we shall call our function as str_cpy ( ).

```
void str_cpy ( char *s1 , char *s2 )
{
        while ( *s2 ! = '\0' )
        {
                *s1 ++ = *s2 ++ ;
        }
```

```
instead you may write :
{
*s1 = *s2 ;
s1 ++ ;
s2 ++ ;
}
```

```
        *s1 = '\0' ;
}
```

```
void main ( )
{
        char str1[100], str2[100] ;
        gets (str2) ;
        str_cpy (str1 , str2 ) ;
        printf ( "%s" , str1 ) ;
```

```
or you may use

puts ( str1 ) ;
```

```
}
```

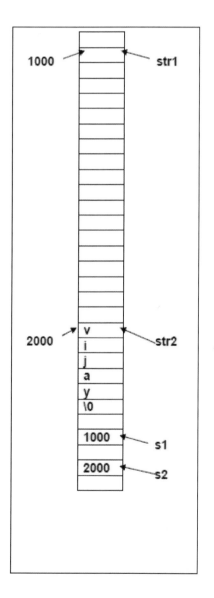

Program to concatenate two strings and put the result in a third string.
Use pointers.

$$(s3 = s1 + s2)$$

We shall call our function as str_cat ( ) since strcat ( ) function is already present in C language.

```
void main ( )
{
        char str1 [50] , str2 [50] , str3 [100] ;
        gets (str1) ;
        gets (str2) ;
        str_cat ( str1 , str2 , str3 ) ;
        puts (str3) ;
}

void str_cat ( char *s1 , char *s2 , char *s3 )
{
        while ( * s1 )
        {
                *s3 = *s1 ;
                s3 ++ ;
                s1 ++ ;
        }

        *s3 ++ = ' ' ;

        while ( * s2 )
        {
                *s3 ++ = *s2 ++ ;
        }

        *s3 = '\0' ;
}
```

> **or use a single statement**
>
> ***s3 ++ = *s1 ++ ;**

> Here we do not say
> *s3 ++ ;
> *s1 ++ ;
> Because we have to increment the pointer and not the content

INSTEAD OF USING WHILE IN THE PREVIOUS PROGRAM, THE SAME CAN BE DONE USING FOR LOOP AS FOLLOWS:

```
void str_cat ( char *s1 , char *s2 , char *s3 )
{
        int i , j ;

        for ( i = 0 ; * ( s1 + i ) ! = '\0' ; i ++ )
        {
                * ( s3 + i ) = * ( s1 + i ) ;
        }

        * ( s3 + i ) = ' ' ;
        i ++ ;

        for ( j = 0 ; * ( s2 + j ) ; j ++ , i ++ )
        {
                * ( s3 + i ) = * ( s2 + j ) ;
        }

        * ( s3 + i ) = '\0' ;
}
```

> If the starting address of str1 is 1000
>   then s1 will point to that
>   which means s1 will contain or hold 1000
>
> If the starting address of str2 is 2000
>   then s2 will point to that
>   which means s2 will contain or hold 2000
>
> If the starting address of str3 is 3000
>   then s3 will point to that
>   which means s3 will contain or hold 3000

STRUCTURE, UNION AND FILES

Files are essentially concerned with a database. To define a record we have to use structures. A structure may be defined as follows:

STRUCTURE

struct employee {
    int no ;
    char name[20] ;
    char qual[10] ;
    float basic_sal ;
    } ;

struct employee emp ;

```
struct employee {
    int no ;
    char name[20] ;
    char qual[10] ;
    float basic_sal ;
    } emp ;
                ←
structure variable name
```

Immediately after defining the structure template a structure variable name has to be specified. Here emp is the structure variable name.

If you want to refer to a member of a structure later in the program, it is referred to as :
        structure variable name . member name
example   emp.no
                 emp.name

UNION

union student {
    int spno ;
    float marks ;
    char name[20] ;
    } stud ;   stud is the union variable name.

In this case for all the members of the union, the starting address or location of the members, in the memory is the same.
IT MEANS YOU CAN USE ANY OF THE MEMBERS IN THE PROGRAM, ONLY ONE AT A TIME.
Program to enter student details and print the result.

```
void main ( )
{
        struct stud_details {
                int spno ;
                char name[20] ;
                int mks1 ;
                int mks2 ;
                int mks3 ;
                int total ;
                float per ;
                char grade[10] ;
                };
        struct stud_details stud[10] ;
        int i ;

        for ( i = 0 ; i < 10 ; i ++ )
        {
                printf ( "\n Enter details of students" ) ;
                scanf ( "%d" , &stud[ i ] . spno ) ;
                scanf ( "%s" , stud[ i ] . name ) ;
                scanf ( "%d" , &stud[ i ] . mks1 ) ;
                scanf ( "%d" , &stud[ i ] . mks2 ) ;
                scanf ( "%d" , &stud[ i ] . mks3 ) ;
        }

        for ( i = 0 ; i < 10 ; i ++ )
        {
                stud[ i ] . total = stud[ i ] . mks1 + stud[ i ] . mks2 +
                stud[ i ] . mks3 ;
                stud[ i ] . per = stud[ i ] . total / 3.0 ;
                if ( stud[ i ] . per > = 75 )
                        strcpy ( stud[ i ] . grade , "distinction" ) ;
                else
                if ( stud[ i ] . per > = 60 )
                        strcpy ( stud[ i ] . grade , "first" ) ;
                else
                if ( stud[ i ] . per > = 40 )
                        strcpy ( stud[ i ] . grade , "second" ) ;
```

```
            else
                    strcpy ( stud[ i ] . grade , "fail" ) ;
        }


        printf ("SPNO NAME MKS1  MKS2  MKS3  TOTAL
        PER  GRADE") ;
        for ( i = 0 ; i < 10 ; i ++ )
        {
                printf ( "%d %s %d %d %d %d %f %s" ,
                        stud[ i ] . spno , stud[ i ] . name , stud[ i ] .
mks1 ,
                        stud[ i ] . mks2 , stud[ i ] . mks3 , stud[ i ] .
total ,
                        stud[ i ] . per , stud[ i ] . grade ) ;
        }
}
```

In this case once the student details are printed and the program is over.....everything is lost...nothing remains in the memory.

If such is required later on for modifications, or adding new student records or for whatever purpose, then we have to get into files....creating files, writing into files....updating files.....reading from files....and so on...all these aspects will come into picture. And since we are concerned with database and consequently records, structures will have to be used.

FILES (Opening, Reading, Creating (Writing) and Closing Files)

fopen ( )   to open a file (file should be existing)
fread ( )   to read from a file (file should be open)
fwrite ( )   to write into a file or create a file
fclose ( )   to close an open file
feof ( )   to check whether end of file is reached
fopen ("filename" , "mode of opening") ;

          "r"   read only
          "w"   write   (create)
          "a"   append (at the end of file)
          "r+"   open for reading / writing / update
          "w+"   open (create) for update also
          "a+"   open (new or existing) for read and
append

To open a file....... A FILE POINTER IS ASSIGNED
THAT FILE POINTER IS USED FOR FURTHER REFERENCING

DEFINING FILE POINTERS

FILE *fp1 , *fp2 ;
Example :

```c
void main ( )
{
        FILE *fp1 , *fp2 ;
        fp1 = fopen ("emp.dat" , "r" ) ;
        fp2 = fopen ("newemp.dat" , "w" ) ;

        if ( ( fp1 = fopen ("emp.dat" , "r" ) ) = = NULL )
        {
                printf ( "File not existing" ) ;
                exit( ) ;
        }
        if ( ( fp2 = fopen ("newemp.dat" , "w" ) ) = = NULL )
        {
                printf ( "Disk full" ) ;
                exit( ) ;
        }
}
```

```
TO CLOSE A FILE....
fclose ( file pointer ) ;
example :
fclose ( fp1 ) ;
fclose ( fp2 ) ;
```

READING FROM AND CREATING (WRITING) INTO FILES:

fread (&buffer , sizeof(buffer) , 1 , file pointer) ;
fwrite (&buffer , sizeof(buffer) , 1 , file pointer) ;
example :
fread (&emp , sizeof (struct employee) , 1 , fp) ;

structure variable name   structure name   no of times to read

CREATE (WRITE) A FILE:

```
void main ( )
{
        struct emp_det {
                int no ;
                char name[20] ;
                char qual[20] ;
                float basic_sal ;
                };
        struct emp_det emp ;
        FILE *fp ;
        int no , i ;
        if ( ( fp = fopen ("emp.dat" , "w" ) ) = = NULL )
        {
                printf ( "\n No Disk Space" ) ;
                exit( ) ;
        }
        printf ( "\n Enter number of employees" ) ;
        scanf ( "%d" , &no ) ;

        for ( i = 0 ; i < no , i ++ )
        {
                printf ( "\n Enter employee details" ) ;

                scanf ( "%d %s %s %f" , &emp.no , emp.name ,
                emp.qual , &emp.basic_sal ) ;

                fwrite ( &emp , sizeof ( struct emp_det ) , 1 , fp ) ;
        }

        fclose ( fp ) ;
}
```

system Vijay M. Vaghela

SIMPLE PROGRAMS ON FILES:

TO READ AND PRINT THE EMPLOYEE DETAILS FILE:

```
void main ( )
{
        struct emp_det {
                int no ;
                char name[20] ;
                char qual[20] ;
                float basic_sal ;
                }
        struct emp_det emp ;

        FILE *fp ;

        if ( ( fp = fopen ( "emp.dat" , "r" ) ) = = NULL )
        {
                printf ( "\n File does not exist" ) ;
                exit( ) ;
        }

        while ( ! feof (fp) )
        {
                fread ( &emp , sizeof ( struct emp_det ) , 1 , fp ) ;
                printf ( "\n %d %s %s %f" , emp.no , emp.name ,
                emp.qual , emp.basic_sal ) ;
        }

        fclose ( fp ) ;

}
```

Explain the steps/ logic that is used, for the following program:

file 1   no , name , qual , basic_sal
file 2   no , allow , dedn

Read the two files which are sorted on number, there are no error conditions, that each corresponding number in file 1 has the same in file 2. Write into a third file which should contain no, name, and net sal.

net salary = basic salary + allowance – deductions

```
void main ( )
{
        struct emp_det {
                int no ;
                char name[20] ;
                char qual[20] ;
                float basic_sal ;
                };
        struct emp_addl {
                int no ;
                float allow ;
                float dedn ;
                };
        struct new_details {
                int no ;
                char name[20] ;
                float net_sal ;
                };

        struct emp_det emp1 ;
        struct emp_addl emp2 ;
        struct new_details emp3 ;

        FILE *fp1 , *fp2 , *fp3 ;

        if ( ( fp1 = fopen ( "emp.dat" , "r" ) ) = = NULL )
        {
```

```
            printf ( "\n File does not exist" ) ;
            exit( ) ;
    }

    if ( ( fp2 = fopen ( "allow.dat" , "r" ) ) = = NULL )
    {
            printf ( "\n File does not exist" ) ;
            exit( ) ;
    }

    if ( ( fp3 = fopen ( "new.dat" , "w" ) ) = = NULL )
    {
            printf ( "\n Disk is full" ) ;
            exit( ) ;
    }

    while ( ! feof ( fp1) )                 Note : you can use fp2
    {
            fread ( &emp1 , sizeof ( struct emp_det ) , 1 , fp1 ) ;
            fread ( &emp2 , sizeof ( struct emp_addl ) , 1 , fp2 ) ;
            emp3.net_sal = emp1.basic_sal + emp2.allow –
            emp2.dedn ;
            emp3.no = emp1.no ;
            strcpy ( emp3.name , emp1.name ) ;

            fwrite ( &emp3 , sizeof ( struct new_details ) , 1 , fp3
            ) ;
    }

    fclose ( fp1 ) ;
    fclose ( fp2 ) ;
    fclose ( fp3 ) ;


}
```

EXAMPLE AND SOLUTION:

File 1 exists and contains no. and other details.
File 2 exists and contains no. and other details.
Both are sorted on number, but some numbers may be missing in both.
Some numbers may be repeating in both.
Write into a third file and this File 3 should contain all the numbers along with other details and should be sorted automatically. If some numbers are repeating in both the files, such numbers should appear only once in the third file.

FILE 1	FILE 2	FILE 3
1	2	1
5	3	2
10	5	3
15	8	5
16	16	8
17	18	10
20	25	15
		16
		17
		18
		20
		25

```
void main ( )
{
        struct emp_det {
                int no ;
                char name [20] ;
                int age ;
                char sex ;
                } ;

        struct emp_det e1 , e2 ;
        FILE *fp1 , *fp2 , *fp3 ;
        fp1 = fopen ( "first.dat" , "r" ) ;
```

```
fp2 = fopen ( "second.dat" , "r" ) ;
fp3 = fopen ( "third.dat" , "w" ) ;

fread ( &e1 , sizeof ( struct emp_det ) , 1 , fp1 ) ;
fread ( &e2 , sizeof ( struct emp_det ) , 1 , fp2 ) ;

while ( ! feof (fp1) && ! feof (fp2) )
{
        if ( e1.no < e2.no )
        {
                fwrite ( &e1 , sizeof ( struct emp_det ) , 1 , fp3
                ) ;
                fread ( &e1 , sizeof ( struct emp_det ) , 1 , fp1
                ) ;
        }
        else
        if ( e1.no > e2.no )
        {
                fwrite ( &e2 , sizeof ( struct emp_det ) , 1 , fp3
                ) ;
                fread ( &e2 , sizeof ( struct emp_det ) , 1 , fp2
                ) ;
        }
        else
        {
                fwrite ( &e1 , sizeof ( struct emp_det ) , 1 , fp3
                ) ;
                fread ( &e1 , sizeof ( struct emp_det ) , 1 , fp1
                ) ;
                fread ( &e2 , sizeof ( struct emp_det ) , 1 , fp2
                ) ;
        }
}
```

```
        if ( feof (fp1) )
        {
                while ( ! feof (fp2) )
                {
                        fwrite ( &e2 , sizeof ( struct emp_det ) , 1 , fp3
                        ) ;
                        fread ( &e2 , sizeof ( struct emp_det ) , 1 , fp2
                        ) ;
                }
        }

        if ( feof (fp2) )
        {
                while ( ! feof (fp1) )
                {
                        fwrite ( &e1 , sizeof ( struct emp_det ) , 1 , fp3
                        ) ;
                        fread ( &e1 , sizeof ( struct emp_det ) , 1 , fp1
                        ) ;
                }
        }
        fclose (fp1) ;
        fclose (fp2) ;
        fclose (fp3) ;
}
```

SAMPLE EXAMPLE PROGRAMS ON FILES:

ATTEMPT THE FOLLOWING PROGRAMS ON YOUR OWN, WITHOUT REFERRING TO THE SOLUTIONS GIVEN:

1)   Write a program to enter data in a MASTER file. It should contain employee number, name, sex and basic.

2)   Write a program to read the data, which has been entered in the MASTER data file which contains the above information of the employees.

3)   Write a program to enter data in a TRANSACTION file. It should contain employee number, allowance and deductions. (When the program is executed, while entering the data in this file, employee numbers should correspond to those entered in the MASTER file.)

4)   Write a program to read the data which has been entered in the TRANSACTION file, which contains employee number, allowance and deductions.

5)   Write a program to read the two files, MASTER and TRANSACTION, which are both sorted on employee number. Find out the net salary of each employee where net = basic + allowance − deductions. Write the records in a new file NEWMAST, which should contain employee number, name and net salary.

6)   Write a program to read the data contained in the NEWMAST file, which contains employee number, name and net salary.

1)   WRITE MASTER FILE

```
#include <stdio.h>
main()
{
    FILE *fp;
    struct mast {
                int empno;
                char name[20];
                char sex;
                float basic;
                } mast_det;

    int no,i;

    if ( (fp=fopen("master.dat","w")) == NULL)
    {
        printf("\n\n File cannot be created");
        exit();
    }
    clrscr();

    printf("\n\n Enter the number of employees ...");
    scanf("%d",&no);

    for(i=1;i<=no;i++)
    {
        printf("\n Enter no, name, sex, basic .. ");
        scanf("%d %s %c %f", &mast_det.empno, mast_det.name,
        &mast_det.sex, &mast_det.basic);

        fwrite(&mast_det, sizeof(struct mast),1,fp);
    }
    fclose(fp);
}
```

2) READ MASTER FILE

```
#include <stdio.h>
void main()
{
    FILE *fp;
    struct mast {
                int empno;
                char name[20];
                char sex;
                float basic;
                } mast_det;


    if ( (fp=fopen("master.dat","r")) == NULL)
    {
        printf("\n\n File cannot be opened");
        exit();
    }

    clrscr();

    printf("\n\n Number Name Sex  Basic");
    while(!feof(fp))
    {
        fread(&mast_det,sizeof(struct mast),1,fp);
        printf("\n%d %s %c %f",mast_det.empno, mast_det.name,
        mast_det.sex,mast_det.basic);
    }
    fclose(fp);
}
```

3)   WRITE TRANSACTION FILE

```c
#include <stdio.h>
void main()
{
    FILE *fp;
    struct trans {
                int empno;
                float allow;
                float dedn;
                } trans_det;

    int no,i;

    if ( (fp=fopen("trans.dat","w")) == NULL)
    {
        printf("\n\n File cannot be created");
        exit();
    }
    clrscr();

    printf("\n\n Enter the number of employees ...");
    scanf("%d",&no);

    for(i=1;i<=no;i++)
    {
        printf("\n Enter no, allowance, deduction .. ");
        scanf("%d %f %f", &trans_det.empno, &trans_det.allow,
        &trans_det.dedn);

        fwrite(&trans_det,sizeof(struct trans),1,fp);
    }
    fclose(fp);
}
```

4) READ TRANSACTION FILE

```
#include <stdio.h>
void main()
{
    FILE *fp;
    struct trans {
                int empno;
                float allow;
                float dedn;
                } trans_det;


    if ( (fp=fopen("trans.dat","r")) == NULL)
    {
        printf("\n\n File cannot be opened");
        exit();
    }

    clrscr();

    printf("\n\n Number  Allowance Deduction");
    while(!feof(fp))
    {
        fread(&trans_det,sizeof(struct trans),1,fp);
        printf("\n%d %f %f", trans_det.empno, trans_det.allow,
        trans_det.dedn);
    }
    fclose(fp);
}
```

5)   WRITE NEW MASTER FILE

```c
#include <stdio.h>
void main()
{
    FILE *fp1,*fp2,*fp3;

    struct mast {
                int no;
                char name[20];
                char sex;
                float basic;
                } m_det;
    struct trans {
                int no;
                float allow;
                float dedn;
                } t_det;
    struct newmast {
                int no;
                char name[20];
                float net;
                } n_det;
    if ( (fp1=fopen("master.dat","r")) == NULL)
    {
        printf("\n\n Cannot open master file ...");
        exit();
    }

    if ( (fp2=fopen("trans.dat","r")) == NULL)
    {
        printf("\n\n Cannot open transaction file ...");
        exit();
    }
```

```
    if ( (fp3=fopen("newmast.dat","w")) == NULL)
{

    printf("\n\n Cannot create New master file ...");
    exit();
}

while (!feof(fp1))
{

    fread(&m_det,sizeof(struct mast),1,fp1);
    fread(&t_det,sizeof(struct trans),1,fp2);

    n_det.net = m_det.basic + t_det.allow - t_det.dedn;
    n_det.no = m_det.no;
    strcpy(n_det.name, m_det.name);

    fwrite(&n_det, sizeof(struct newmast), 1, fp3);

}
fclose(fp1);
fclose(fp2);
fclose(fp3);
}
```

6)   READ NEW MASTER FILE

```c
#include <stdio.h>
void main()
{
    FILE *fp;

    struct newmast {
                    int no;
                    char name[20];
                    float net;
                } n_det;

    if ( (fp=fopen("newmast.dat","r")) == NULL)
    {
        printf("\n\n Cannot read New master file ...");
        exit();
    }

    clrscr();
    printf("\n\n Number Name Net");
    while (!feof(fp))
    {
        fread(&n_det, sizeof(struct newmast), 1, fp);
        printf("\n %d %s %f",n_det.no,n_det.name,n_det.net);
    }
    fclose(fp);
}
```

MORE PROGRAM EXAMPLES IN C FOR PRACTICE

Program to convert decimal to binary.
eg. 45 = 101101

```
# include <stdio.h >
void main ( )
{
        int a[50], ctr = 0, x, no;
        printf ("\n Enter the number in decimal ... ");
        scanf ("%d", &no);
        x = no;

        while ( x > 0 )
        {       a[ctr] = x % 2 ;
                ctr++ ;
                x /= 2;
        }
        printf ("\n The binary equivalent of decimal %d is ",no);
        while ( ctr > 0 )
        {
                printf ("%d", a[ctr-1] );
                ctr- - ;
        }
}
```

Program to generate Fibbonaci series upto n terms :
eg. 1   1   2   3   5   8   13   . . . .

```
#include <stdio.h>
void main ( )
{
        int i , f1 = 1 , f2 = 1 , sum = 0 , no;
        printf ("\n Enter the number of terms");
        scanf ("%d", &no);
        printf ("\n\nThe fibbonacci sequence upto %d terms is",no);
        printf("%d,%d", f1 , f2);

        for ( i = 3 ; i <= no ; i++)
        {
                sum = f1+f2;
                f1 = f2 ;
                f2 = sum ;
                printf (",%d", sum) ;
        }
}
```

**Input a number and a string, put the string, number times, each time a new
line with 1 space indent.**
eg. 10, Vijay

ouput　　Vijay
　　　　　Vijay
　　　　　　Vijay
　　　　　　　Vijay

．．．．．．．．．．

```
#include <stdio.h>
void main( )
{
    int no, i, j ;
    char name[20];

    printf ("\n Enter the string") ;
    gets (name);

    printf("\n Enter the number of times the string is to be printed ");
    scanf("%d",&no);

    for (i = 1; i <= no; i++)
    {
        printf("\n");
        for (j = 1; j < i;  j++)
            printf(" ");
        printf("%s",name);
    }
}
```

Given an array of integers, print whether the array is sorted or not.

```c
# include <stdio.h>
void main ( )
{
        int a[50] , i , no , f1 = 0, f2 = 0 ;

        printf ("\n Enter the number of elements") ;
        scanf ("%d" , &no) ;

        for ( i = 0 ; i < no ; i++)
        {
                printf ("\nEnter element number %d in the array", i +
                1);
                scanf ("%d" , &a[i] ) ;
        }

        for ( i = 0 ; i < no -1 ; i++)
        {
                if ( a[ i ] > a[ i+1 ] )
                   f1++;
                if ( a[ i ] < a[ i+1 ] )
                   f2++;
        }
        if (f1 == 0)
           printf ("\n The array is sorted in ascending order") ;
        else
           if (f2 == 0)
                printf("\n The array is sorted in descending order");
           else
                printf ("\n The array is not sorted") ;
}
```

Input an integer number and find its divisors.
eg. 36 = 1, 2, 3, 4, 6, 9, 12, 18, 36

```c
# include <stdio.h>
void main ( )
{
        int i , no ;

        printf ("\n Enter the number to be checked") ;
        scanf ("%d" , &no) ;

        printf ("\n The divisors of %d are", no) ;

        for ( i = 1 ; i <= no ; i++)
          if ( no% i = = 0 )
                printf ("%5d" , i) ;
}
```

Find the sum of the following series :
$$1!/x - 3!/x^3 + 5!/x^5 - 7!/x^7 \ldots. \text{ upto n terms}$$

```
#include <stdio.h>
void main( )
{
    int i, k = 1, sign = 1, no;
    float sum = 0, num = 1, den, x;

    printf("\nEnter the value for x ... ");
    scanf("%f",&x);

    printf("\nEnter the number of terms of the series .. ");
    scanf("%d",&no);

    den = x;

    for (i = 1; i <=no; i++)
    {
            sum  + =  num/den*sign;
            num  * =  (k+1)*(k+2);
            den  * =  x * x;
            k    + =  2;
            sign * =  -1;
    }
    printf("The sum of the series is %f",sum);
}
```

Program to generate the following output:

          1
        121
     12321
   1234321

```c
#include <stdio.h>
void main( )
{
   int j,k = 1;
   long a = 1,i = 0;

   while ( k++ <= 4 )
   {
     i = i*10 + 1;
     a = i * i;

     printf("\n");
     for (j = 40; j >= k; j- -)
          printf(" ");
     printf("%ld",a);
   }
}
```

Find the largest and second largest of a set of n numbers. DO NOT use arrays.

```c
# include <stdio.h>
void main ( )
{
    float lar, lar2 , temp , c ;
    int no , i ;
    printf ("\n Enter how many numbers") ;
    scanf ("%d", &no) ;
    printf ("\n Enter numbers 1 and 2") ;
    scanf ("%f%f", &lar, &lar2) ;
    if (lar2 > lar)
    {
        temp = lar ;
        lar = lar2 ;
        lar2 = temp ;
    }
    for ( i = 3 ; i <= no ; i++ )
    {
        printf ("\n Enter number %d" , i ) ;
        scanf ("%f" , &c) ;
        if ( c > lar2)
        {
            temp = lar2 ;
            lar2 = c ;
            c = temp ;
            if ( lar2 > lar)
            {
                temp = lar ;
                lar = lar2 ;
                lar2 = temp ;
            }
        }
    }
    printf ("\n The largest number is %8.2f", lar) ;
    printf ("\n The second largest number is %8.2f", lar2) ;
}
```

Find the common divisors of 2 integers entered via the keyboard.
eg. 36 & 45 = 1, 3, 9

```c
# include <stdio.h>
void main ( )
{
        int i , no1, no2, temp ;

        printf ("\n Enter the first number .. ") ;
        scanf ("%d" , &no1) ;
        printf ("\n Enter the second number .. ");
        scanf ("%d",&no2);

        printf ("\n The common divisors of %d and %d are ",
        no1,no2);

        if (no1 > no2)
        {
            temp = no1;
            no1 = no2;
            no2 = temp;
        }

        for ( i = 1 ; i <= no1 ; i++)
           if ( no1%i = = 0 && no2%i = = 0)
                printf ("%5d" , i) ;

}
```

Find the sum of the series $1^1 + 2^2 + 3^3 + 4^4 + 5^5 \ldots$ upto n terms.

```c
#include <stdio.h>
void main( )
{
    int i, j, sum = 0, temp, no ;

    printf("\nEnter the number of terms of the series .. ");
    scanf("%d",&no);

    for (i = 1; i <= no; i++)
    {
        temp = 1;
        for(j = 1; j <= i;  j++)
            temp * =  i;
        sum + =  temp;
    }
    printf("The sum of the series is %d",sum);
}
```

Program to generate the following output :

```
        1
       2 2
      3 3 3
     4 4 4 4
    5 5 5 5 5
```

```c
#include <stdio.h>
void main( )
{
    int no, x = 40, i, j ;

    printf("\n Enter the number of lines ... ");
    scanf("%d",&no);

    for (i = 1; i < = no; i++)
    {
        printf("\n");
        for (j = x; j > 0; j- -)
            printf(" ");
        x - - ;
        for(j = 1; j <= i; j++)
            printf("%2d",i);
    }
}
```

Multiply two integer numbers without using multiplication.

```
# include <stdio.h>
void main ( )
{
        int i , no1, no2, sum = 0 ;

        printf ("\n Enter the first number .. ") ;
        scanf ("%d" , &no1) ;
        printf("\n Enter the second number .. ");
        scanf("%d",&no2);

        for ( i = 1 ; i <= no1 ; i++)
           sum + = no2;
        printf ("The product of %d * %d = %d " , no1,no2,sum) ;
}
```

*   *   *   *   *   *   *

BEST WISHES FOR ALL THE SUCCESS IN LEARNING AND
UNDERSTANDING THIS SUBJECT, C PROGRAMMING,
REMAIN WITH ALL THE READERS, TEACHERS AND
STUDENTS WHO HAVE REFERRED TO THIS CONTENT.

Vijay M. Vaghela

Practical C Programming Examples

PRACTICAL
Programming
EXAMPLES

Practical C Programming Examples

Printed in Great Britain
by Amazon

17268312R00063